THE CHRISTMAS TRUCE OF 1914

Essential Library

An Imprint of Abdo Publishing
abdopublishing.com

ESSENTIAL LIBRARY OF
WORLD WAR I

BY TOM STREISSGUTH

CONTENT CONSULTANT

JASON MYERS, PHD
INDEPENDENT SCHOLAR

abdopublishing.com

Published by Abdo Publishing, a division of ABDO, PO Box 398166, Minneapolis, Minnesota 55439. Copyright © 2016 by Abdo Consulting Group, Inc. International copyrights reserved in all countries. No part of this book may be reproduced in any form without written permission from the publisher. Essential Library™ is a trademark and logo of Abdo Publishing.

Printed in the United States of America, North Mankato, Minnesota

102015
012016

Cover Photo: Press Association/AP Images
Interior Photos: Press Association/AP Images, 1; Everett Historical/Shutterstock Images, 4, 43, 72, 77, 85, 89; Sammlung Sauer/Picture-Alliance/DPA/AP Images, 8; The Print Collector/Heritage Images/Glow Images, 11, 14, 16, 52; AP Images, 18, 98 (top left); General Photographic Agency/Getty Images, 23; Bain News Service/Library of Congress, 29, 30, 36, 39, 48, 51, 55, 98 (top right), 98 (bottom); Red Line Editorial, 35; Daily Mirror/Mirrorpix/Corbis, 44; Stapleton Historical Collection/Heritage Images/Glow Images, 56; Imperial War Museums (Q 11745), 59; Science and Society/SuperStock, 62; Rosseforp/ImageBroker RM/Glow Images, 66; Underwood Archives/Getty Images, 70; Hulton-Deutsch Collection/Corbis, 74; Leemage/UIG/Getty Images, 78; Library of Congress, 80; US Marine Corps History Division, 82, 99; W. L. King/Library of Congress, 90–91; Photo 12/UIG/Getty Images, 93; Subel Bhandari/EPA/Corbis, 95; Phil Noble/Reuters/Corbis, 97

Editor: Melissa York
Series Designers: Kelsey Oseid and Maggie Villaume

Library of Congress Control Number: 2015945636

Cataloging-in-Publication Data

Streissguth, Tom.
 The Christmas Truce of 1914 / Tom Streissguth.
  p. cm. -- (Essential library of World War I)
ISBN 978-1-62403-921-8 (lib. bdg.)
Includes bibliographical references and index.
1. Christmas Truce, 1914--Juvenile literature. 2. World War, 1914-1918--Campaigns--Juvenile literature. 3. World War, 1914-1918--Armistices--Juvenile literature.   I. Title.
940.4/21--dc23

CONTENTS

Belgian troops marched to defend their country in 1914.

PEACE BREAKS OUT

World War I (1914–1918), known to those who fought it as the Great War, began in Europe during a spell of fine midsummer weather. Armies numbering in the millions marched to the front lines, while civilians on all sides cheered them on and prayed for a swift victory. French and English troops faced German infantry in Belgium and northern France. Germany invaded Russian-occupied Poland. Heavy guns behind the lines provided cover for daytime assaults. As the war dragged on into the fall, the battles on the western front turned into a stalemate.

It was the assassination of an Austrian prince in the early summer of 1914 that started the diplomatic crisis that led to war. After six weeks of threats, the Central powers—Germany, Austria-Hungary and the Ottoman Empire—went to war with the Allies of the United Kingdom, France, and Russia. On the western front, neither side could gain any ground, but neither side would agree to a peace. On the eastern front, Germany and Russia took heavy casualties in a series of fierce battles.

Soldiers began digging trenches as the German advance came to a halt. These seven-foot- (2 m) deep ditches ran in zigzag lines stretching hundreds of miles across northern France and Belgium. In addition to the frontline trenches, communication trenches were used by messengers and to resupply the frontline troops. Other trenches sheltered the wounded. A century later, in northern France and Belgium, visitors can still see long depressions in the land, marking the place where men lived, fought, and died for four years.

Along the front, gunfire usually stopped when dusk fell over the lines. Artillery spotters, who located targets for the heavy guns, couldn't work in the dark. Airplanes and balloons were grounded. Snipers stayed on the firing steps, which allowed them to see over the front edge of their trenches. They peered over the parapets for any flash of light from the enemy positions. Their best targets were scavengers looking to strip the dead of their clothing and weapons or rescue parties working between the lines in the dark.

In some places, the trenches were no more than 100 yards (90 m) apart. With their specialized binoculars that could be extended above the edge of a trench, the men could easily follow lights that appeared on the other side. Noises traveled well when the air was still. One could easily hear an enemy's clattering cooking pot or the thump of an ammunition box set down heavily on the ground. Yet even if a head did appear above the parapet, there was a tendency at night, among most soldiers, to live and let live. Everyone needed sleep, and officers rarely ordered suicidal night assaults.

Daily life in the trenches was often cold, wet, and thoroughly miserable for all ranks. Rains flooded the makeshift barracks and small dugouts built into the trench sides. Even in dry weather, these dark holes were unpleasantly cold, humid, and dark. Floors were of dirt or sometimes planked over with thin wooden walkways known as duckboards. It was difficult to keep food out of the dirt and away from the ravenous rats. Fleas and lice tormented soldiers.

In the first months of the war, an informal truce often took hold at daybreak and during mealtimes. Men would occasionally come out of their trenches

COLD, WET FEET

Although they were designed to protect infantry from heavy artillery, snipers, and machine gun fire, the trenches of the western front could be miserable and unhealthy places. Rainy days were common in northern France and Belgium, and winters could be long, cold, and damp. The water that collected in the trench bottoms soaked into the leather boots worn by soldiers. Many of them came down with trench foot.

Foot tissue breaks down when feet remain wet for a long time. Blisters form while the skin turns red and becomes itchy and swollen. Without treatment or better conditions, the skin and underlying muscles lose circulation and die. In the worst cases, trench foot means the loss of toes and sometimes the entire foot.

Soldiers hunted rats for sport and self-defense.

under a white flag signifying a truce to barter cigarettes, rations, and other valued items with the enemy. Newspapers, once finished, were flung across no-man's-land. It was common at these times for opposing sides to trade banter and taunts. Occasionally, patriotic songs could be heard from the enemy's trench.

But the veneer of civilization was thin in wartime, especially under the conditions of trench warfare. Cold weather, boredom, and the constant threat of horrible injury or sudden death forced soldiers to leave behind the common courtesies of politeness and respect. Men on both sides were hungry and often sick. Ernst Jünger, a German officer, recalled:

BRITISH RATIONS

Over the long course of World War I, the British army had to feed more than 2 million men serving on the front lines in Belgium and France.[1] Officially, the rations were supposed to provide British soldiers with 4,000 calories a day, but the food was often so poor the men could barely eat it. As the war dragged on, the rations for the frontline soldiers grew smaller; by 1916, only six ounces of "bully beef" were provided a day. English soldiers changed the French word *bouilli*, or "boiled," to "bully" to describe this canned meat.

Along with the beef, a soldier in the trenches could expect a daily ration of hard biscuits and bread. When the flour ran short, the bread was made from turnips. Another common dish was maconochie, a thin stew of vegetables cooked in a beef broth. Bacon, cheese, and jam were provided occasionally, and British soldiers also held to the tradition of daily tea. Along with the cold and damp conditions and the danger from enemy snipers, the poor food and unhealthy water were among the worst aspects of a soldier's life in the trenches.

Rations, too, were very poor. Beyond the thin midday soup, there was nothing but the third of a loaf, and something infinitesimal to eat with it, usually half-mouldy jam. Most of mine was always eaten by a fat rat, for which I often lay in wait, but in vain.

This sparse living, which left us always half-fed, brought about a most unpleasant state of affairs. The men often suffered literally from hunger, and this led to pilfering of rations. When it comes to food, the good manners that in Europe are mostly whitewash are soon scratched off. Privations and danger tear away all that has been acquired, and then good form survives only in those in whom it is born.[2]

In some sectors, soldiers on both sides kept hostilities to a minimum. Around the massive fortifications of Belfort, France, for example, the French had manned their lines with older army veterans. These men understood early in the war that the two sides had reached a stalemate. They had little enthusiasm for combat across no-man's-land. On the other side, German troops kept quietly to their trenches as well. Their officers knew even if they could mount an effective assault, their advance would eventually be halted and thrown back by Belfort's heavy guns.

As the war continued, volunteers completed their training and arrived at the front. Many of the veterans who fought at the start of the war were killed, rotated out of the front lines, or released from duty for serious injuries. New recruits came with determination for the fight and rushed into no-man's-land as their officers ordered massive assaults on enemy positions. Officers on both sides of the war threatened courts-martial for disobeying orders or for fraternization with the enemy.

ACTION AT PLOEGSTEERT WOOD

Nevertheless, the war was not a constant battle. On many days, only snipers were firing across no-man's-land. Along the western front, troops from the Allies and the Central powers raised white flags whenever they sought a temporary truce. Cease-fires occurred at mealtimes, or when one side wanted to rescue their

Troops on both sides used lulls in the fighting to retrieve wounded and dead comrades.

wounded or bury their dead. Officers observed these friendly episodes with alarm and ordered them to stop. A British general, G. T. Forrestier-Walker, announced that such fraternization:

> *Discourages initiatives in commanders, and destroys the offensive spirit in all ranks. Friendly intercourse with the enemy, unofficial armistices and the exchange of tobacco and other comforts, however tempting and occasionally amusing they may be, are absolutely prohibited.*[3]

British officers believed a bit of action would help stem the tide of brotherly feeling. In November, the British army suffered heavy losses during the fighting in and around the Belgian town of Ypres, not far from the North Sea coast. As the French army moved in to reinforce the British, French officers pressured their British colleagues to stage another offensive and retake the initiative.

The British officers studied their maps of the Ypres Salient, a bulge in the line where Allied troops were exposed to German guns from three sides. The countryside was as flat as a tabletop. In rainy weather, the trenches filled with mud and miserably cold water. There were few obstacles, such as hills or wide rivers, that could be used for defense. The British found a likely spot for II Corps, a large division of the army, to stage a renewed assault on the German lines at Ploegsteert, a small Belgian village with an adjoining forest just north of the French border.

On December 19, 1914, the Eleventh and Twenty-Second Brigades of II Corps began an advance just east of Ploegsteert Wood. Small groups of men climbed over the trench parapets and rushed across no-man's-land. They were met by heavy machine gun and rifle fire from the German side. Although the British were supported by artillery, many of them were killed or wounded when their own shells fell short of the German positions. The British were easily thrown back, leaving behind hundreds of dead as well as wounded men screaming for help.

Firing ceased when German units positioned opposite the Twenty-Second Brigade agreed to assist wounded British soldiers lying in no-man's-land. This occurred in many places along the western front during the war. At a signal, enemy troops would agree to hold their fire when wounded men were helped back to their own lines, or soldiers came out to bury the dead. There were no formal truces, however, and officers had the authority to court-martial any man for slacking.

THE SIGNAL FOR A TRUCE

In many sectors of the western front, both sides came to an understanding. In a letter home, a British telegraph operator, Andrew Todd, explained the truce system:

Perhaps it will surprise you to learn that the soldiers in both lines of trenches have become very "pally" with each other. The trenches are only 60 yards [55 m] apart at one place, and every morning about breakfast time one of the soldiers sticks a board in the air. As soon as this board goes up all firing ceases, and men from either side draw their water and rations. All through the breakfast hour, and so long as this board is up, silence reigns supreme, but whenever the board comes down the first unlucky devil who shows even so much as a hand gets a bullet through it.[4]

Winter brought increasingly cold and uncomfortable conditions in the trenches.

At Ploegsteert, German snipers picked off several British soldiers who were trying to carry the wounded from the battlefield.

THE FIRST TRUCE OF THE SEASON

Truces along the line increased in the next few days after Ploegsteert. A hard frost that began in the week before Christmas made it easier to navigate on foot over the mud and through shell holes. Near the French town of Armentières, German troops passed a cake to the British lines, and with it an invitation to attend a Christmas concert under a cease-fire. The appointed time was 7:30 p.m. The signal would be men from both sides simply putting their heads above the trenches.

Armentières was an unlikely place for a sudden outbreak of peace. It occupied a key point along the line near the English Channel coast, and it was the scene of frequent skirmishes between British and German troops. The city lay due south of Ypres and just over the border from Belgium. The trenches ran just east of the city. On December 14, German artillery had bombarded the town. Hundreds of houses were damaged or destroyed, and smoking rubble filled the streets. Several hundred shells landed on or near the city's hospital, used by British troops for lodging when they rotated out of the line for rest. The city was also frequently attacked from the air.

In the countryside, the shelling targeted farmhouses along the battle lines and in no-man's-land. Although these country homes and barns had been abandoned, they still provided cover for snipers. They were also storehouses for rations and ammunition. Very few buildings of any kind positioned near the trenches survived the war. Headquarters units were set up well behind the lines, where officers and staff were safe from shelling and sniper fire.

Christmastime in 1914 brought feelings of peace and fellow feeling even to soldiers in the trenches.

Sergeant John Minnery described the night of December 24:

> On Christmas Eve, the Germans were shouting and singing in their trenches, which were only about 50 yards or 60 yards [45 or 55 m] from ours. Our chaps sung and shouted back to them, and about midnight one of the Germans called out "Will one of yours come and meet me?" "Yes," we replied, "if there is no shooting." "There is to be no shooting," he answered, and I went out to meet him after our sentries got orders not to fire.[5]

The British responded politely to the offer of a Christmas concert, sending over a small packet of tobacco in token of their acceptance. Lights came on, and the truce went ahead through the evening hours without further hostilities. As small groups of German troops broke into song, they invited the British to sing along. Finally, after the patriotic anthem "Die Wacht am Rhein" ("The Watch on the Rhine") was heard from the German trench, lights were extinguished and both sides ended the concert with shots fired into the sky.

A few kilometers to the north, lighted Christmas trees positioned on the edges of the German trenches drew scattered fire from the British, who believed a night assault was about to take place. Quiet prevailed through the night, however, and early on Christmas a thick fog descended over the countryside. A German officer, Lieutenant Johannes Niemann of the 133rd Saxon Regiment, described what happened next:

> Next morning the mist was slow to clear and suddenly my orderly threw himself into my dugout to say that both German and Scottish soldiers had come out of their trenches and were fraternizing along the front. I grabbed my binoculars and looking cautiously over the parapet saw the incredible sight of our soldiers exchanging cigarettes, schnapps and chocolate with the enemy. Later a Scottish soldier appeared with a football.[6]

The Christmas truce of 1914 had begun.

Archduke Franz Ferdinand and his wife, Sophie, walk to their car on the day of the assassination.

THE GREAT WAR

The spark that ignited World War I occurred six months earlier, on June 28, 1914. On that day, Archduke Franz Ferdinand and his wife, Sophie, climbed into an open touring car to visit the city of Sarajevo. Franz Ferdinand was the heir of Franz Joseph I, emperor of Austria. The archduke often scheduled short visits to the far-flung outposts of the empire, including this bustling capital of Bosnia, a province of Austria-Hungary.

As Franz Ferdinand knew, there was real danger in visiting Sarajevo. The city was home to many of his sworn enemies, including men who were willing to kill for the cause of the Slavic peoples—including Serbs, Macedonians, Croats, and Slovenes—governed by Austria-Hungary. Opponents of the Hapsburgs, the dynasty that had ruled Austria since the 1200s, these insurgents wanted a united, independent Slavic nation: Yugoslavia.

Gavrilo Princip, 19 years old, was just one of many insurgents. A short and slight man, he was the son of a poor family from independent Serbia, which bordered Austria-Hungary. Committed to the cause of Yugoslavia, he had been given weapons by the shadowy Black Hand organization for an attack on the archduke in Sarajevo. On June 28, while sitting at a café, he spotted the car carrying the royal couple as it turned into a nearby street. Princip rushed over to the car, pulled out his Browning FN pistol, and fired two shots point-blank at the archduke and his wife. Both died within minutes.

The murders touched off a storm of protest from Austria-Hungary's leaders, who accused Serbian officers of giving weapons and instructions to Princip and several other conspirators in Sarajevo. On July 23, Austria delivered an ultimatum to Serbia, demanding that the Serbian government cooperate with an Austrian investigation into the

THE BLACK HAND

Political turmoil and war in the Balkans in the early 1900s gave rise to the Black Hand organization. Also known as the Union of Death, the Black Hand carried out murders and terrorist acts to achieve the union of Slavic peoples in the Balkan region of Europe. Several of its leaders were high-ranking ministers in the government of independent Serbia; a group of these men plotted the assassination of Archduke Franz Ferdinand. The murder touched off World War I, which caused millions of deaths but ultimately brought about the creation of Yugoslavia, or "Union of South Slavs."

assassination. Before the deadline for a response had passed, Austria-Hungary ordered its army to mobilize for an invasion.

The political upheaval in the Balkans dragged in the great powers of Europe. The emperor of Austria called on his ally Germany for help. Russia, Serbia's ally, had promised to protect Serbia in any conflict with Austria-Hungary. But Nicholas II, the czar of Russia, had no desire to fight Austria-Hungary, Germany, or any other nation over trouble in the Balkans. On July 29, Nicholas sent an urgent coded telegram to his third cousin, Kaiser Wilhelm II, the ruler of Germany:

> *I foresee that very soon I shall be overwhelmed by the pressure forced upon me and be forced to take extreme measures which will lead to war. To try and avoid such a calamity as a European war I beg you in the name of our old friendship to do what you can to stop your allies from going too far.*[1]

THE CRISIS OF 1914

There had been violent conflict in the Balkans for centuries, and two wars had been fought in the region since 1900. The nations of Greece, Serbia, Macedonia, and Bulgaria were all involved, but the major powers stayed out. By the summer of 1914, however, many leaders in Germany and Austria-Hungary believed a war with their European rivals was inevitable—even desirable—to shift the European balance of power in their favor. Kaiser Wilhelm's military leaders had spent the last 20 years making plans to fight France as well as Russia. In their view, an alliance of these two states posed a dire threat to Germany's existence.

Nicholas and Wilhelm exchanged a flurry of telegrams in the next few days. Nicholas had no interest in war and no desire to seize territory or defeat Germany's armies. If Russia had to declare war, Nicholas hoped to fight only Austria-Hungary. But the czar also believed that not mobilizing on all fronts would leave Russia exposed to an invasion from Austria-Hungary or Germany, or both. The czar did not realize Austria-Hungary was committing half of its army to Serbia. With only 50 percent of its army available, Austria-Hungary was not strong enough to invade Russia or Russian-occupied Poland on its own.[2]

Russia was vast. If war came, its armies would have to move quickly to meet the German and Austrian forces at the western border. Upon declaration of war, the Russian armies would gather across a nation the size of a continent, climb aboard thousands of passenger trains, and head west. There would be nothing Nicholas could do to stop the mobilization once it started.

Many factors were pushing the great powers of Europe into a world war. Austria-Hungary wanted to extend its control over the Balkan region by smashing Serbia. Both Germany and Austria-Hungary wanted to fight Russia before the Russians could modernize their military forces. The czar felt an obligation to protect the Serbs, who shared ethnic ties, as well as the Orthodox Christian religion, with Russia. Germany wanted to hold Alsace-Lorraine, the

Kaiser Wilhelm, *left*, and Czar Nicholas, *right*, met on multiple occasions before World War I, although the third cousins did not entirely trust each other.

territory it had won from France in the Franco-Prussian War of 1870. France wanted to recapture this region, but it could not match Germany's military might without help from the United Kingdom.

The British government watched the crisis on the European continent unfold. The United Kingdom had only a small land army, but it was home to the world's most powerful navy. The empire had colonies all over the world, including India, Burma, and British East Africa (modern Kenya), as well as armies to occupy and control these colonies. But the British had not prepared for war across the European landmass, and it had not fought in Europe for more than half a century.

British leaders had pledged to defend France in case of attack by Germany. The Treaty of London, dating back to 1839, promised to protect the small nation of Belgium. At the same time, Belgian leaders were trying to keep their country neutral in these big-power conflicts. Ruled by King Albert I, Belgium had not signed any treaties with Germany or France. It could muster only a small army of 117,000 men.[3] To defend their territory, the Belgians were forced to rely on

THE PROBLEM WITH TREATIES

The world's major powers signed several military alliances in the years leading up to 1914. Germany, Austria, and Italy signed the Triple Alliance in 1882. In response, Russia and France signed a mutual defense pact in 1891. The British and Japanese formed a naval alliance in 1902, Britain signed the Entente Cordiale with France in 1904, and Russia joined the Entente in 1907. Although the intention of these treaties was to keep the peace, all of these countries were simultaneously building up their military forces. In 1914, the web of pacts, treaties, and alliances dragged many nations into a confrontation in which they had no real quarrel with their enemies. The result was World War I.

outdated weapons, a few cavalry regiments, and two powerful fortresses in the cities of Liège and Namur. Germany had no interest in the permanent conquest of Belgium. But unfortunately for the Belgians, their country lay directly between Germany and France.

A CALL TO ARMS

The German generals wanted to avoid a two-front war against Russia and France. Well before the outbreak of war in 1914, they had drawn up the Schlieffen Plan, which had the bulk of German armies invading France. A smaller force would protect Germany's eastern front against Russia. Once the French were defeated, the victorious German army would move to the eastern front to greet the Russians, whom the German general staff believed would be slower to mobilize.

Nicholas II of Russia was not a decisive or confident ruler. While he resisted the demands of his ministers to declare war in support of Serbia, he was eventually persuaded to order a mobilization of the Russian army. On July 29, he reconsidered and canceled the order. On the next day, he changed his mind again, and Russia called up its troops. That decision would have disastrous consequences for the czar and the Russian Empire.

France also wanted to avoid war with Germany. The French generals planned only to defend their frontiers. They did not want to take the offensive against the German army. As the war loomed, French units were ordered to take up positions six miles (10 km) from the borders with Belgium and Germany. French officers hoped this would avoid any incidents that might bring about a German invasion.

Mobilization all over Europe was the occasion for celebration, parades, patriotic songs, and newspaper editorials supporting the decision to go to war.

In Paris, France; Berlin, Germany; and Vienna, Austria, soldiers paraded through the streets with rifles and full gear, enjoying the admiration of the crowds. In each country, people believed they were fighting for national survival against enemies who wished to destroy their families and their way of life. The French also saw the war as a chance to avenge their defeat in the Franco-Prussian War. Austrians wanted Serbia to pay for the assassination of Franz Ferdinand.

Across the English Channel, British leaders began making preparations of their own. The British army issued orders to reserve soldiers to report to their regiments. Even horses and automobiles were called up. Men had just a day or

SOLDIERS ON PARADE

In Schneidemühl, Prussia, a young girl watched an infantry regiment board a train for the front. She later recorded the scene in her diary:

Then the 149th marched up shoulder to shoulder and streamed onto the platform like a grey tidal wave. All the soldiers had long garlands of flowers around their necks or pinned on their breasts. Asters, stocks and roses stuck out of the rifle barrels as if they were intending to shoot flowers at the enemy. The soldiers' faces were serious. I had expected them to be laughing and exultant.[4]

two to bid farewell to their work, their families, and their civilian life. People on all sides began realizing this would be a "great war," stretching across Europe and perhaps even reaching far-flung colonies in Africa and Asia.

German leaders believed they had to act quickly to prevent an attack by their enemies. In the last week of July 1914, the Schlieffen Plan was put into effect. The German army sent hundreds of infantry, artillery, and cavalry divisions to its western borders shared with Belgium and France. On August 2, Germany delivered an ultimatum to Belgium. The kaiser demanded that the Belgian government allow German armies to cross Belgian territory. As justification, the message falsely claimed the French were planning to invade Belgium.

The Belgian government was given 24 hours to respond to the ultimatum. A refusal would be considered an act of war. In a speech in Berlin, Kaiser Wilhelm declared, "A fateful hour has fallen upon Germany. Envious people on all sides are compelling us to resort to a just defense. The sword is being forced into our hands."[5] On August 4, German troops crossed the border.

In the United Kingdom, leaders of the global empire believed their nation benefited from a careful balance of power in Europe. The British government did not want to see Germany or Britain's ancient rival, France, dominate the continent. Nor did they want to see the German army controlling the other side of the English Channel, just a few miles from southern England. British honor was also at stake: the 1839 Treaty of London guaranteed the British would protect Belgium if Germany attacked.

Although the British hesitated for several days, the government declared war after Germany ignored the United Kingdom's demand to retreat from Belgium. Prime Minister Herbert Asquith would eventually defend the British government's decision: "We are fighting to vindicate the principle that small nationalities are not to be crushed, in defiance of international good faith, by the arbitrary will of a strong and overmastering Power."[6] Poor communications, diplomatic miscalculation, a complicated web of treaties and alliances, and national pride were turning the assassination of an Austrian archduke in a small Bosnian city into one of the most destructive wars in history.

FIGHTING WHILE YOUNG

The official policy of the British army set a minimum age of 18 for new recruits. For frontline service, the minimum age was 19. But at the start of war, the United Kingdom faced a serious manpower shortage. The German army numbered more than 3 million while the British could muster only 700,000.

British recruiters were paid for each man they enlisted, and the military was not always strict about age requirements. As a result, more than 250,000 underage teenagers fought on the western front for the British armies. Of this number, approximately half were killed, wounded, or taken prisoner by the war's end in 1918.[7]

KAISER WILHELM II

1859–1941

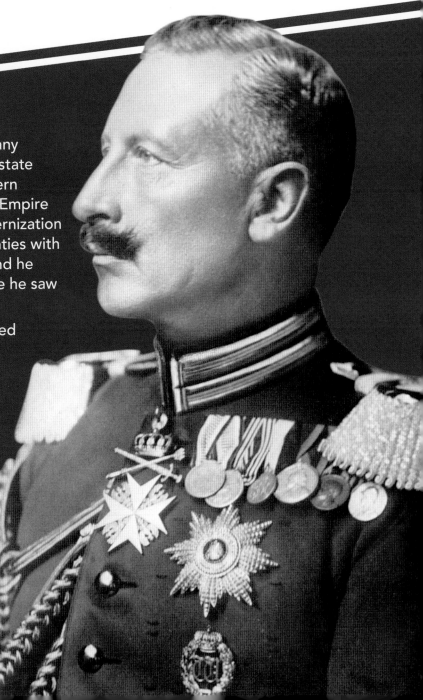

After the Franco-Prussian War in 1870, Germany had ambitions to become the most powerful state in Europe. Kaiser Wilhelm II of the Hohenzollern dynasty, who took the throne of the German Empire in 1888, ordered a massive buildup and modernization of the German army and navy. He signed treaties with Austria-Hungary and the Ottoman Empire, and he actively sought conflict with Russia, an empire he saw as Germany's chief rival.

Wilhelm was a strict ruler who often clashed with his ministers, including the powerful Otto von Bismarck, chancellor of Germany, whom Wilhelm forced from office in 1890. The emperor's great admiration for military leaders was tinged with envy—his withered left arm, damaged at birth, prevented strenuous exercise or physical activity. Many historians believe Wilhelm's frustrated ambition for military glory played an important role in Germany's declaration of war in 1914 and the outbreak of World War I.

German troops had taken control of Brussels, the Belgian capital, within two weeks of the invasion.

APPEALS FOR PEACE

German war planners sent seven armies—more than 1 million men—to the western front.[1] Thousands of trains steamed across the Rhine River, near the border of France and Germany. The trains halted to unload soldiers, horses, and tons of equipment, guns, and ammunition. The Central powers of Germany, Austria-Hungary, and the Ottoman Empire began their march to war against the Allies: the United Kingdom, France, Russia and—later in the war— Italy and the United States.

The war on the western front began with a German invasion of Belgium on August 4, 1914. The German generals sought to fight through the French lines and then head south for Paris. With the capital in danger, the Germans believed the French would quickly agree to peace terms. Only one thing stood in Germany's way:

Belgium, still a neutral country, lay on the path to northern France. The Belgians thought their strongholds at Antwerp, Liège, and Namur would protect their country. Liège alone had 12 separate forts, 400 heavy guns, and a garrison of 20,000.[2]

The British government delivered an ultimatum as soon as Germany invaded Belgium: German armies must retreat from Belgium immediately. Even if the United Kingdom did decide to back up its promise to Belgium with troops, German leaders thought the British could do little to stop a German advance, knowing the British land army was quite small.

When Germany failed to heed the British ultimatum, the British government immediately declared war. The British admiralty, under the leadership of Winston Churchill, sent out a war telegram to all ships to begin hostilities against Germany. In France, the government called for a general mobilization. To many French citizens, the coming of war was thrilling. The excitement of being locked in a contest of strength and will with Germany, France's historic enemy, inspired parades in cities and towns all over France. At the same time, the sense of excitement was mixed with dread for many families. Husbands, fathers, and brothers marched off to join their units. French sergeant Marc Bloch of the 272nd Infantry Regiment, who later won renown as a medieval historian, recalled:

One of the most beautiful memories the war has given me was the sight of Paris during the first days of mobilization. The city was quiet and somewhat solemn. The drop in traffic, the absence of buses, and shortage of taxis made the streets almost silent. The sadness that was buried in our hearts showed only in the red and swollen eyes of many women.[3]

Marshal Joseph Joffre, commander of the French army, ordered a counterattack to the east against Alsace. The idea was to break through to the Rhine River and cut off the German armies sweeping through Belgium. As the

PROMOTING THE WAR

Max Aitken was a young Canadian who served for a time as a journalist on the western front. He moved back to England during the war. Through his connections in the British government he won the title of Lord Beaverbrook, as well as an appointment as minister of propaganda.

Beaverbrook's mission was to convince the public to support the war effort. He commissioned artists to create striking posters. Well-known writers, including Rudyard Kipling and H. G. Wells, wrote pro-war pamphlets and articles. Beaverbrook invented the photographic recruiting poster and was the first producer of movie newsreels in the United Kingdom. He encouraged newspapers to prominently feature good news from the western front and downplay the severe hardships and dangers faced by the troops. After the war's end, Beaverbrook gained ownership of two prominent British papers, the *Express* and the *Evening Standard*. With these outlets, he carried on the work of war propaganda after the outbreak of World War II in 1939.

situation developed, the French government wanted to take the offensive against the Germans, believing this would be the best way to keep the war short while regaining the provinces lost to Germany in 1870 and 1871.

The Germans had set up strong defensive positions on the hilly, forested terrain of the region, which strained communications for the French units. French infantry, still wearing their brightly colored nineteenth-century uniforms, began their advance in the first week of the war. German machine guns mowed them down by the thousands.

In Belgium, the German armies rushed through lightly defended cities and surrounded the strongholds at Liège and Namur as they moved toward their ultimate goal, Paris. General Alexander von Kluck, commander of the German First Army, was determined to crush the French infantry positioned northeast and east of Paris, along the Marne River.

The French and British drove into a 12-mile (19 km) gap between the German First and Second Armies. The commander of the French Sixth Army, Joseph-Simon Gallieni, ordered 1,200 Parisian taxi drivers to bring their vehicles to the capital's busy train stations for a crucial task.[4] Driving from the city by the hundreds, the cabs delivered desperately needed reinforcements to the Marne front. The German armies were unable to close the gap.

By mid-September, the German armies retreated behind the Marne River and began raising a long series of fortifications to prevent any further breakthroughs

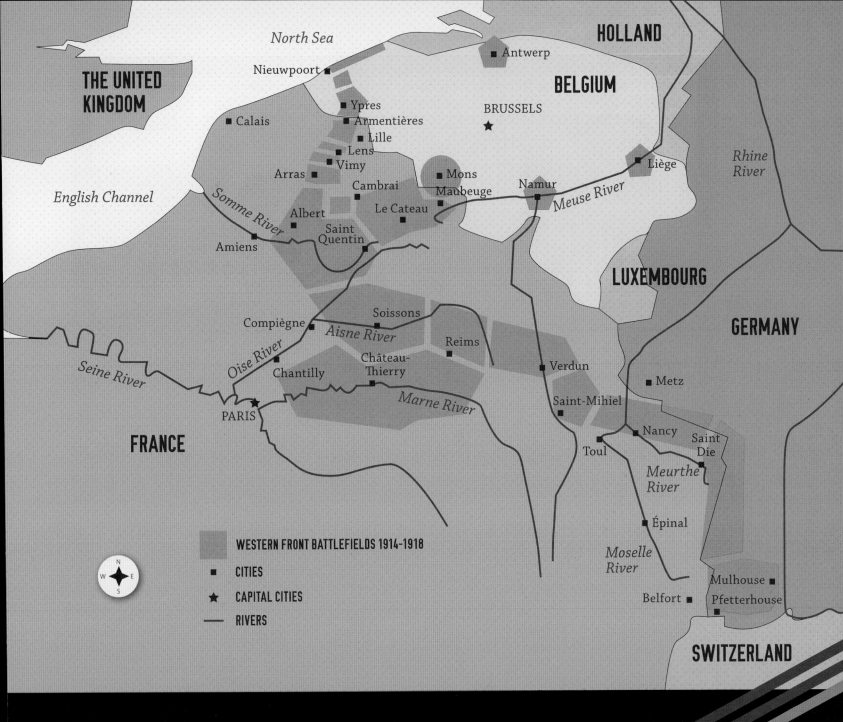

North Sea

THE UNITED
KINGDOM

HOLLAND

Nieuwpoort ■

Antwerp ■

BELGIUM

BRUSSELS
★

Calais ■

Ypres ■
Armentières ■
Lille ■
Lens ■
Vimy ■

Arras ■

Cambrai ■

Mons ■
Maubeuge ■

Namur ■

Liège ■

Rhine
River

English Channel

Somme River

Albert ■
Saint
Quentin ■

Le Cateau ■

Meuse River

LUXEMBOURG

Amiens ■

GERMANY

Compiègne ■

Soissons ■

Aisne River

Reims ■

Verdun ■

Seine River

Oise River

Chantilly ■

Château-
Thierry ■

Metz ■

Saint-Mihiel ■

Marne River

PARIS ★

Nancy ■
Saint
Die ■

FRANCE

Toul ■

Meurthe
River

Épinal ■

Moselle
River

WESTERN FRONT BATTLEFIELDS 1914-1918

■ CITIES

Belfort ■

Mulhouse ■
Pfetterhouse ■

★ CAPITAL CITIES

— RIVERS

N
W E
S

SWITZERLAND

Parisian taxis joined the war effort by delivering soldiers to battle.

by the Allies. Both armies extended their lines west to the city of Lille. Further west, at Ypres, the British took up positions in a series of trenches running north and south across Flanders, a region straddling the French-Belgium border. The British fortified the ports of Dunkirk and Boulogne, which provided a lifeline to supplies and reinforcements from the United Kingdom.

Western Belgium was a flat, damp region where groundwater lay close to the surface, and a system of canals, dams, and dikes prevented flooding by North Sea water. Rain quickly flooded the trenches and turned the roads to muddy streams. In late October, the Germans attacked the British lines with reinforcements from the recently captured city of Antwerp. The German advance continued until October 29, when a group of Belgian sappers opened the sluice gates at Nieuwpoort, flooding the countryside and making offensive operations impossible. The flooding of a huge swath of Flanders allowed the British and French armies to reorganize and take up stronger defensive positions.

The result was a halt to the German advance and a stalemate all along the western front. Because of heavy losses on both sides, many experienced veterans were soon out of combat. Toward the end of the year, informal truces became much more common.

A GENERAL PREPARES FOR CHRISTMAS

With the Christmas season approaching, General Sir Horace Smith-Dorrien of the British Expeditionary Force saw a clear danger. On December 5, he issued a stern order, explaining,

> It is during this period that the greatest danger to the morale of troops exists. Experience of this and of every other war proves undoubtedly that troops in trenches in close proximity to the enemy slide very easily, if permitted to do so, into a "live and let live" theory of life . . . such an attitude is however most dangerous for it discourages initiative in commanders and destroys the offensive spirit in all ranks. . . . Friendly intercourse with the enemy, unofficial armistices, however tempting and amusing they may be, are absolutely prohibited.[5]

Battle began on the eastern front when Russia staged an invasion of East Prussia, a province of Germany, on August 17. Under the leadership of Paul von Hindenburg and Erich Ludendorff, the outnumbered German army mounted a powerful counterattack. At the battle of Tannenberg, German troops fought their way past the Russian Second Army, taking tens of thousands of prisoners. A week later, another Russian defeat took place at the battle of Masurian Lakes in eastern Poland. Although the Russians later stopped an invasion of southern Poland by the Austrian army, poor communications put the Russian generals at a serious disadvantage on the eastern front.

CALLS FOR PEACE

The war in Belgium and northern France continued through the fall of 1914. Many people on both sides had believed the conflict would end by Christmas. In earlier European wars, winter often put a stop to military offensives. Cold and snow always slowed the movement of troops. When snow began to fall, armies at war had to provide shelter for their equipment, men, and horses.

This time, however, the war dragged on through the fall months without letup, causing death and hardship across a wide swath of France and Belgium. As the German army advanced, it committed atrocities against the civilian population. If Belgian snipers attacked the German troops, German officers ordered immediate reprisals against civilians. The troops killed men, women, and children who were taking no part in the war. Heavy shelling reduced the university city of Louvain, with its renowned library and great cathedral, to ruins.

The British press ran front-page stories of murder, looting, and rape taking place in Belgium. The accounts shocked readers, who expected a more orderly and civilized war. In the British media, the German troops became the Huns, ravenous and murderous barbarians who had to be stopped by any means possible. The publicity surrounding the civilian deaths in Belgium boosted British enlistment and helped politicians in the United States who called for their own country to get involved.

A German soldier's winter gear gave him some protection against the elements.

By December 1914, the armies on the western front had reached a stalemate. French, German, and British troops were digging trench lines that stretched almost 500 miles (800 km), from the North Sea to Switzerland. These trench lines would remain in place, moving very little for the next four years.

A few leaders in neutral countries made appeals for peace. In the United States, Senator William Kenyon of Iowa put forward a resolution in favor of a 20-day cease-fire over the holidays. Pope Benedict XV, leader of the Catholic Church, asked the warring nations to agree to a truce over the Christmas season. The truce would begin on December 7 and give the leaders a chance to negotiate a more permanent peace.

The German government announced it would accept the truce if its enemies did. The Russian government, however, refused to cooperate. The Orthodox calendar used by the Russian church set Christmas on January 7, nearly two weeks later than the Catholic and Protestant Christmas. Russians, therefore, could not recognize a truce that assumed Christmas Day as taking place on December 25.

DISILLUSIONED WITH WAR

Sigmund Freud, the renowned psychologist from Vienna, had supported Austria's mobilization against Serbia. Within a few months of the start of the conflict, he changed his opinion:

Then the war in which we had refused to believe broke out, and it brought— disillusionment. Not only is it more bloody and more destructive than any war of other days, because of the enormously increased perfection of weapons of attack and defence; it is at least as cruel, as embittered, as implacable as any that has preceded it.[6]

PEACE AT CHRISTMAS

Along the front lines, many soldiers knew the story of a Christmas peace that occurred during the Franco-Prussian War nearly 50 years before. Near the French town of Saint Cloud, French and German armies were fighting on Christmas Eve. After dark, the bells of Saint Cloud's church tower began ringing out a traditional Christmas melody. On both sides of the line, the firing stopped without any warning or announcement. Soldiers on both sides began singing Christmas carols. The concert continued for an hour past midnight. At dawn, the two armies were fighting again.

Important changes had taken place in technology, and transportation, and military science since the Franco-Prussian War. Telegraph communications had become commonplace. Rail networks allowed much faster passage of armies from one sector to another, and motorcars allowed for fast personal transport. Artillery guns were larger and more

THE INTERNATIONAL LANGUAGE

Many tales of the Christmas truce describe how it began with both sides joining in a Christmas carol. "Silent Night," for example, was known as "Stille Nacht" in German, and when German troops sang "Adeste Fidelis," the British responded with "O Come All Ye Faithful." The German folk song "O Tannenbaum" was familiar to all sides in World War I, as were rousing patriotic songs such as "Tipperary" and "Die Wacht am Rhein." For a day or two, the international language of music helped thousands of troops from many different nations communicate peacefully.

accurate, aircraft allowed reconnaissance and bombing from the air, and well-placed machine guns could easily stop a cavalry charge.

Many people believed these new technologies would bring the war to a rapid conclusion, or that a decisive battle would eventually force one side or the other to sue for peace. Another common view was that if the war dragged on too long, government leaders would realize their armies had reached a stalemate and they were making a pointless sacrifice of their men and resources. When that happened, a truce would bring all sides to the negotiating table. Surely a war begun on such a thin pretext could be easily resolved.

Larger and more accurate artillery was one factor that made World War I deadlier than previous wars.

The British government hoped its Princess Mary gift boxes would help keep up troop morale over the holiday season.

THE CHRISTMAS SEASON

The nations at war had not forgotten Christmas. King George V and Queen Mary of the United Kingdom sent holiday cards to every man at the front. The British government also arranged to send Princess Mary boxes across the English Channel to Europe. Named for the 17-year-old daughter of the royal couple, these small brass tins held a greeting card, a photograph of the princess, a small pipe, a bit of tobacco, and cigarettes. If the soldier didn't smoke, he received a package of sweets and a small pencil with a metal holder in the shape of a bullet cartridge. Nurses at the front received chocolate. By Christmas Day, the supply units on the western front handed out more than 355,000 Princess Mary boxes.[1]

German soldiers received candy, clothing, cakes, and tobacco, as well as thousands of Christmas trees. For the German troops, Christmas was an especially important holiday, deeply embedded in the culture for centuries. At the edge of the German trenches, small Christmas trees brightened the short days and long nights of December.

THE KAISER PLANS TO BOOST MORALE

As the war dragged on through the fall of 1914, Kaiser Wilhelm II of Germany grew concerned about the troops on the western front. As a morale-boosting measure, the kaiser ordered 100,000 Christmas trees to be delivered to the front lines for the holidays.[3] For several days, German supply trains were loaded with fresh-cut evergreens. After the trees reached depots near the front, they were unloaded and shipped in wagons to the trenches. The Kaiser may have believed the Christmas trees would boost his soldiers' fighting spirit, but they had a very different effect on Christmas Eve, when German soldiers set up the trees on their parapets and invited English and French soldiers to take part in a holiday truce.

British and German officers still would not allow any official truces. Many believed gift-giving, singing, and any kind of celebration would be out of place while the fighting continued. Captain Rudolf Binding of the German army wrote to his father:

> *If I had my way some person in authority would proclaim that Christmas will not be celebrated this year. . . . Enemy, Death and a Christmas tree—they cannot live so close together.*[2]

With the precision of a military campaign, trains brought boxcar loads of gifts, letters, and Christmas cards to

ANCIENT OBSERVANCES

German soldiers on the western front carried on a national tradition by placing small trees on the edge of their trenches. According to many historians, the Germans were the first to bring trees into their homes at the time of the winter solstice, which occurs in December just a few days before Christmas. The winter solstice was an important holiday. In Germany, the tradition of lighting candles on trees dates back to pre-Christian times.

The pagan ancestors of the Germans were forest-dwelling people, some of whom worshiped trees and other natural features. The tradition of lighting trees was adapted to Christianity as religious conversion took place throughout northern Europe. The popular Queen Victoria, ruler of the United Kingdom through much of the 1800s, is given credit for bringing this tradition to the English.

depots near the front. In some places, the ordinary movement of soldiers and equipment was disrupted. Storing and distributing gifts to every single man in the front lines tied up supply wagons and warehouses. Major G. D. Jeffrys of the British Second Grenadier Guards made this diary entry on December 18:

> *Everything seems hung up just now for all the Christmas parcels, which are becoming a positive nuisance. . . . It seems rather ridiculous to make such a tremendous business of it when, after all, our first business is to beat the Germans. Our enemy thinks of war, and nothing else, whilst we must mix it up with plum puddings.*[4]

All sides were still committed to victory. The British sought to tear down Germany's military superiority in Europe. The people of Germany believed

Gifts arrive for German soldiers.

their existence as a nation was under threat. Austria still wanted revenge on Serbia. France and Belgium wanted reparations for the war's cost in soldiers and material and for the many ruined cities and civilian deaths in their territories.

The weather turned colder as the holiday approached. Fields of mud turned to barren, frozen ground. There were no major offensives, and informal cease-fires became more common. Men came out for burial details or to rescue the wounded. In some sectors, mealtimes provided a daily occasion for a temporary truce.

Cease-fires also occurred on the eastern front, even in distant colonies where small detachments of English and German soldiers were carrying on hostilities. Tanga, a seaport in German East Africa, was one of many colonial outposts where British and German officers agreed to a truce. Richard Meinertzhagen, a British officer, wrote,

> *It seemed so odd that I should be having a meal today with people whom I was trying to kill yesterday. It seemed so wrong and made me wonder whether this really was war or whether we had all made a ghastly mistake.*[5]

German officers knew their own troops would be inclined to give the war a rest at Christmas. The problem arose from the German war strategy. Most of the seasoned German soldiers and older, toughened veterans had been sent to the Russian front. Younger and less experienced soldiers who were recruited first, or who quickly volunteered, boarded trains for the western front. Likewise, in the United Kingdom, young men rushed to join the war for the personal glory they thought they might achieve. Many acted out of fear the war might end before they could get to the front. As the war dragged on through the fall of 1914, however, youthful enthusiasm faded. The horror of combat and the dreariness of life in soggy, rat-infested trenches brought war-weariness to many soldiers on both sides.

THE TRUCE BEGINS

On Christmas Eve 1914, the young German soldier Karl Muhlegg, a member of the Seventeenth Bavarian Regiment, climbed out of his trench and walked to an army depot in Langemarck, Belgium. He found a row of small Christmas trees that had been shipped to the front from Germany. Muhlegg bought a small pine with Christmas candles already attached and returned to his position. He was exposed to enemy rifles and machine guns for part of the way. But Muhlegg was unharmed, as he wrote in a letter:

> *After all, I was Father Christmas bearing a decorated tree, although with a gun over my shoulder and a bag of ammunition! I handed the captain the little Christmas tree. . . . He lit the candles and wished his soldiers, the German nation and the whole world "Peace according to the message from the angel." Never was I as keenly aware of the insanity of war.*[6]

Around the Ypres Salient, near Lille in northern France, and in several other sectors of the western front, soldiers signaled to their opponents they were coming out unarmed. Where the trenches were close enough together, they shouted Christmas greetings across the lines. After going over the parapets, they met in no-man's-land, introduced themselves, and exchanged small gifts.

West of Lille, the Second Scots Guards faced the German Fifteenth Westphalian. This regiment was one of several, including the Black Watch,

German soldiers gather around a Christmas tree.

recruited from Scottish volunteers. Just a week before, on December 18,
a furious battle in the same place had left dozens of men lying dead in
no-man's-land. The Scots were scheduled to rotate out of the line for rest and
leave. As they pulled together their weapons and equipment and began filing to
the rear, singing erupted from the German trench. The Scots Guards could hear
the music of a brass band and Christmas greetings shouted across no-man's-land.

A singing competition broke out. The Scots sang "It's a Long Way to
Tipperary," a British military tradition. The Germans replied with "God Save the

ALFRED ANDERSON

1896–2005

On Christmas Eve 1914, an 18-year-old member of the Scottish Black Watch Regiment listened carefully to something unusual: silence. For the next day, the Christmas truce gave Alfred Anderson's unit a rest from the almost constant noise of heavy artillery, rifles, and machine guns. Writing home, he described the strange episode:

> All I'd heard for two months in the trenches was the hissing, cracking and whining of bullets in flight, machine gun fire and distant German voices. But there was a dead silence that morning, right across the land as far as you could see. We shouted 'Merry Christmas,' even though nobody felt merry. The silence ended early in the afternoon and the killing started again. It was a short peace in a terrible war.[7]

Anderson lived longer than any other British, French, or German veteran of the Christmas truce. He was 109 years old when he died in 2005, one of the world's last living World War I veterans and the oldest man in Scotland.

King," then "Tipperary" sung in German. The lines were approximately 80 yards (70 m) apart, and men on both sides had to raise their voices to be heard. The competition continued, then finished with all sides singing "Auld Lang Syne" in unison. On the next day, men from both sides emerged without their weapons. A German officer announced a truce to continue until 1:00 p.m. so both sides could bury their dead.

British infantryman Archibald Henry Buchanan-Dunlop described events in a letter home:

> *Even out here this is a time of peace & goodwill. I've just spent an hour talking to the German officers & men who have drawn a line halfway between our left trenches & theirs & have all met our men and officers there. We exchanged cigars, cigarettes, & papers. They are jolly, cheery fellows for the most part, & it seems so silly under the circumstances to be fighting them.*[8]

LAST BATTLE OF 1914

The French army had suffered heavy losses by early December 1914. Although the German drive to Paris had been stopped, the French could not mount a coordinated offensive. French commanders relayed a request to the British: attack the Germans in western Flanders. They hoped this would force the Germans to move reinforcements from other parts of the line, taking the pressure off the French.

Despite the poor winter weather, the British commanders eagerly sought a chance at a breakthrough. On December 19, at just past 3:00 a.m., a division of Indian troops under British command moved out near the French town of Givenchy. The division advanced across the barren fields and seized 300 yards (270 m) of enemy trench.

The Germans regrouped, gathering their retreating infantry and moving machine guns for a counterattack. On the morning of December 20, a heavy artillery bombardment fell on the Indian troops. The Germans moved in with bayonets fixed and hand grenades ready. Mines placed by German sappers detonated underneath the British lines.

The British offensive at Givenchy was halted. Several thousand men had been killed or wounded, and the British had gained no ground. The futile attack angered the Indians, who found the wet and cold conditions of northern Europe hard to tolerate. Many of these units were already on the brink of mutiny. To protect the army's general morale, their officers rotated most out of the front lines.

Hundreds of dead and wounded still lay strewn throughout no-man's-land. Both sides called a general truce just before Christmas to retrieve their casualties from the

Soldiers from India fought in France under British command.

battlefield. According to one historian, "The burial of many bodies of comrades lying in the frost and bloody pools of no-man's-land was one of the motivations for the Christmas fraternization that soon occurred in this area."[9]

The arrival of letters and packages from home was always cause for celebration for the men in the trenches.

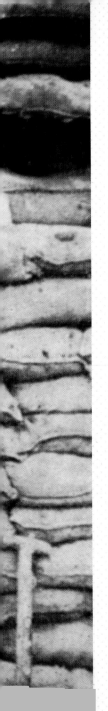

CHRISTMAS MEALS AND SOCCER MATCHES

The Christmas Eve truce spread along the western front. Similar truces took place in Eastern Europe among Germans and Russians. Soldiers had a few hours or even days of peace.

Many took the chance to write letters home. Censors carefully screened the letters to ensure they revealed nothing that could help the enemy. Through these letters, news of the truce began to reach home. One Englishman described how,

> *An informal compact was arranged . . . to the effect that no sniping was to take place for a day. In consequence, out of their burrows came English and Germans alike, and commenced to hang out their washing and mend their wire entanglements.*[1]

BARTER AND BUTTONS

By meeting the enemy peacefully in no-man's-land, many British troops temporarily lost their dread and hatred of Germans. Halfway between the trenches, the men from the two sides gave each other small items such as cigarettes and buttons. Even when the language barrier prevented communication, the two sides were willing to trade goods. A favorite of the Germans was the bully beef and the apple-and-plum jam British soldiers regularly received from home. The British could also offer their tins of maconochie vegetable stew. In exchange, some German units were able to offer barrels of beer, which were rolled toward the British trenches. The British sought military souvenirs, including buttons, belt buckles, and the traditional spiked helmet, known as the pickelhaube, worn by German officers.

Men shook hands and exchanged addresses. Some of them brought cameras and took photographs. No weapons were present. The soldiers exchanged information about their lives before the war. Many Germans had worked in

WRITING TO THE FRONT

Letters and parcels sent to the western front, especially during the Christmas season, put a serious strain on the British postal system. In the days before radio and personal phones were in common use, most people got their information by letters, and there was no more welcome arrival in the trenches than a stamped and sealed envelope from home. In a single week in December 1914, the British post office accepted 200,000 parcels and 2.5 million letters.[2]

British and German troops met at Ploegsteert, Belgium, during the truce.

the United Kingdom before the war, and it was common for young Germans to speak English as a second language. Some had business or personal contacts with British citizens too.

Near Ypres, four unarmed Germans approached the commander of the Scots Guards regiment, Captain Edward Hulse. "Their spokesman started off by saying that he thought it only right to come over and wish us a happy Christmas," wrote Hulse in a letter home, "and trusted us implicitly to keep the truce. He came from Suffolk [England], where he had left his best girl and a 3-1/2 h.p. motorbike!"[3]

On January 4, 1915, the *Bristol Evening News* printed a letter from a Private Field, who had encountered,

> *One small, grubby and ill-shaven German, who had a few words of English. I asked him if he had ever been to England and he said, "no, but I am clerk; I business with England." "What is your business?" I asked, and I shrieked with joy as he gravely said "exporters of mouth organs."[4]*

HUMAN BEHAVIOR

The Christmas truce has served historians and scientists with material for their study of human behavior in a battlefield environment. Biologist Robert Sapolsky, for example, studied incidents including the Christmas truce to find patterns of cooperation between enemies common to humans and other species:

> One side might get their best sniper to put a bullet into the wall of an abandoned house near enemy lines. Then he would do it repeatedly, hitting the same spot. What was being communicated? "Look how good our guy is. He could have aimed at you, but chose not to. What do you say to that?" And the other side would reciprocate with their best sniper. What had just started? An agreement to shoot over each other's heads.[5]

On the German side, enthusiasm about the war varied. The country had only recently been united into a single nation, but there remained regional and ethnic divisions. Most men from Saxony and Bavaria were not professional soldiers. They were volunteers and recruits who were not as committed to the war. However, Prussians in general made fierce and dedicated soldiers; the Prussian army had led the assault on France in 1870. Saxons and Bavarians were often hostile to the Prussians and their traditional culture of military discipline.

As an Allied letter writer observed,

> The Germans opposite us were awfully decent fellows—Saxons, intelligent and respectable-looking men. I had quite a decent talk with three or four, and have two names and addresses in my notebook. It was the strangest scene you can imagine—going out unarmed to meet our enemies, also unarmed. After our talk I really think a lot of our newspaper reports must be horribly exaggerated. Of course these men were Saxons, not Prussians.[6]

Many of the English and German soldiers understood the war was futile, premised on an insignificant quarrel that did not really concern either of their respective nations. There was no German threat to British territory, although there was fighting in East Africa where British and German colonies bordered each other. For some, the entire war seemed to be nothing more than a royal family quarrel—Kaiser Wilhelm was the grandson of Queen Victoria, the cousin

British soldiers celebrated Christmas with a special meal.

of the British King George V, and the third cousin of Czar Nicholas—for which commoners were fighting and dying by the millions.

There remained some places along the front where officers obeyed the ban on fraternizing with the enemy. The enlisted men remained in their trenches and the lines remained silent. There were also places where officers accepted the truce without an order from their commanders and came out quietly with the enlisted men. As Captain Charles "Buffalo Bill" Stockwell of the Royal Welch Fusiliers recalled of the cease-fire that occurred in his sector:

> *Things were getting a bit thick. . . . My men were getting a bit excited. . . . We did not like to fire as they were all unarmed, but we had strict orders and someone might have fired, so I climbed over the parapet and shouted, in my best German, for the opposing Captain to appear.*[7]

Stockwell and the German commander met in no-man's-land. With great formality, the officers shook hands and introduced their aides. It was customary, at such a time, to offer gifts. The German officer rolled out a barrel of beer, and in exchange Stockwell offered a traditional English plum pudding. While the men talked, the lines remained peaceful. A German aide appeared to set up glasses for the gathered men and pour out bottles of beer.

In abandoned homes and barns, small groups of men gathered to share a meal. Wild rabbits, which abounded in northern France, provided the meat.

> "I had a go at the ball. I was pretty good then, at 19. Everybody seemed to be enjoying themselves. There was no sort of ill-will between us. There was no referee, and no score, no tally at all. It was simply a melee—nothing like the soccer you see on television. The boots we wore were a menace—those great big boots we had on—and in those days the balls were made of leather and they soon got very soggy."[9]
>
> *—Recollections of British private Ernie Williams of Christmas 1914 near Wulverghem, Belgium, given on the BBC program* Grandstand *in 1983*

A few Germans even invited their British enemies behind their lines, promising that no harm would come to them. Instead of squatting uncomfortably in trenches and dugouts, the men enjoyed a civilized dinner in a house at a table, with wine and champagne to accompany the meal. Good food and comfortable surroundings were a rare prize during wartime.

TRUCE GAMES

The English and the Germans shared a love of sports, especially soccer. The two countries often took part in friendly international contests. They now carried that tradition to peaceful battlefields in France and Belgium on Christmas Day. A German soldier, Lieutenant Kurt Zehmisch, recorded in his diary,

> A couple of Britons brought a ball along from their trenches, and a lively game began. How fantastically wonderful and strange. The English officers experienced it like that too—that thanks to soccer and Christmas, the feast of love, deadly enemies briefly came together as friends.[8]

The soccer matches between British and Germans during the Christmas truce became legendary. From one side or the other, a leather ball would appear. Goals were set up with a pair of boots or a stake driven into the ground. Few men watching were able to hold back, and at one point, so the stories go, several hundred men were taking part in one game.

THE SOCCER DEBATE

Many letters sent home by British troops in January 1915 mention soccer matches that were played between enemy troops. Not all historians believe the story, however. In an interview with news network CNN, Professor Mark Connelly of the University of Kent said,

> There is no absolute hard, verifiable evidence of a match. . . . I think it highly likely that someone, somewhere did bring out a ball and a bit of a kick about took place, but that is a long, long way from saying it definitely happened and that it was anything like a formal match rather than just men tapping a ball about. . . . Truces are very common in war and often involve both sides ignoring each other in order to carry out common tasks— often burial of dead and retrieval of wounded. At Christmas 1914 where the truce occurred most men took part in it in this tacit manner rather than actively fraternized, which is clearly much more 'romantic' and appealing.[10]

The winter of 1914–1915 saw much uncomfortable fighting in the trenches.

CARRYING ON THE FIGHT

Not every sector saw a Christmas truce. There were cease-fires where French armies faced the Germans, but these events saw less fraternization between the two parties. The French saw the war as a defense of their homeland against a German occupation. German guns were destroying French cities and killing French civilians. In these circumstances, there was much less chance of enemies trading gifts or enjoying friendly games of soccer.

Fighting also continued in some British sectors with the encouragement of officers who insisted on strict discipline in the trenches. The Second Battalion of the Grenadier Guards, positioned at the southern end of the British line near Ypres, exchanged heavy fire with the Germans on Christmas Eve. The next morning the Germans called out from their trenches, proposing a holiday truce. They were met by another attack. Sniping between the trenches continued throughout Christmas Day. Captain William Congreve of the Third Infantry Division, stationed near the town of Kemmel, Belgium, reported a similar incident in his diary:

> We have issued strict orders to the men not on any account to allow a "truce." As we have heard they will try to. The Germans did try. They came over toward us singing. So we opened rapid fire on them, which is the only sort of truce they deserve.[1]

A PAUSE TO BURY THE DEAD

Even on Christmas, burial details were solemn occasions. Because no-man's-land was so dangerous, many bodies remained exposed where they fell for weeks at a time. Troops on both sides felt a need to put their dead to a permanent rest. In the *Manchester Courier*, one British soldier recounts the gruesome task, which he carried out not far from a group of Germans on a similar mission:

> *English and German returned for spades, and between us we gave decent burial to those poor fellows who had fallen weeks previously, and who had, perforce, to be abandoned on the field. We had tried on several occasions to get out to these bodies and bury them by night, but such a procedure always resulted in shots being exchanged and a hasty return whence we came.*
>
> *But today I stood shoulder to shoulder with a German and dug a grave for his late comrade. Crosses now mark the spot where for weeks there had lain three gruesome forms.[2]*

Congreve and other officers on both sides were under orders to allow no fraternization, whether or not a holiday was taking place. Since there was no formal truce, confusion reigned in several places. Scattered rifle fire broke up peaceful meetings between British and German troops. A few men who came out under a flag of truce were killed by ricocheting bullets, fired from distant positions. A British soldier who brought a gift of cigarettes to the German lines was shot as he approached. The Germans from that position immediately sent an apology message across no-man's-land.

Even where there was no fraternization with the enemy, many locations saw the guns go quiet for Christmas. For many units, the temporary lull in fighting presented a useful opportunity to reinforce their positions. Men were sent out into no-man's-land to repair the barbed wire that protected their trenches from a massed infantry attack. Both sides sent spies across to get a better look at supply depots and gun positions.

As the sounds of battle were replaced by an eerie silence, ammunition and food were brought up from the rear. Men worked in the freezing weather to drain their trenches and repair collapsed dugouts. Many wrote letters home, while others hunted rats for sport. Officers consulted their maps and made note of enemy troop concentrations. Their goal was to improve the accuracy of their shelling in the new year.

Others enjoyed a holiday leave back in the United Kingdom. Only 70 miles (110 km) lay between Ypres and the English coastal city of Dover, where on some nights it was possible to hear the noise of detonating mines from across the English Channel. Enlisted men and officers who were fighting in muddy trenches one day were home with their families the next, enjoying the company of parents, wives, and children. They sat down to peaceful meals, took walks, attended the theater, and enjoyed a good night's sleep for the first time in months. But troubling memories of fighting, fear, and violent death still haunted many. To discuss war with people who had no experience of it seemed impossible.

German soldiers repairing a telegraph line, 1915

BATTLES RESUME

For those on the front lines who enjoyed a peaceful Christmas, the coming of night meant the war was on again. Many units had arranged signals, such as rifle shots or overhead flares, to let troops on both sides know the day of peace was over. In eastern France, during the afternoon of Christmas Day, General Joffre ordered two divisions of infantry to mount an attack through the hilly, forested Vosges region. The French goal was to take control of a rail line used by the Germans for reinforcements. Fighting grew hot around the town of Steinbach, where French and German troops carried on merciless house-to-house fighting.

A truce scheduled to last until midnight in the Picardy region, northeast of Paris, gave the French the chance for a surprise attack thanks to a difference in timekeeping. Clocks ran one hour ahead on the German side of the line. French sappers set a massive underground mine timed to

SPEAKING AGAINST THE WAR

In December 1914, a group of British women sent an "Open Christmas Letter" to the women of Germany and Austria. The letter asked their support for a general cease-fire and peace talks. The letter was the work of Emily Hobhouse, a British antiwar activist.

Wartime laws in the United Kingdom banned communicating directly with Germany, so Hobhouse sent the Open Christmas Letter to newspapers in the United States. In the spring of 1915, German and Austrian women answered the letter with their own peace message. Many supporters of women's suffrage called for an international peace conference at which neutral nations would help the nations at war reach the terms of a permanent truce. Despite these efforts, the war continued for three more years.

In some places, nighttime gunfire signaled the end of the truce.

explode at precisely 11:45 p.m.—45 minutes after midnight, by the German's reckoning. The official diary of the French Fifty-Sixth brigade recorded:

> *Immediately a detachment rushes forward to take possession of the crater and exploit the incident, but the enemy, being on the alert, greets them with rocket flares, hand grenades and above all rifle fire. Finally they execute a counter-attack and our detachment withdraws with some difficulty using the bayonet.*[3]

The day following Christmas, by the British calendar, was Boxing Day. This was a day set aside for giving small gift boxes to household workers and servants. Many units on both sides continued holding their fire. Men who had seen four straight months of violence and death were not eager to pick up their rifles again. In a few places, the truce continued a full week, until the new year.

Just as the truce had begun with informal agreements, so it ended. German, British, and French military traditions included some common courtesies. After a truce, either declared or informal, rifle shots into the air provided the signal for fighting to resume, warning the troops to clear out of no-man's-land. In some places, men scrambled out of their trenches at the last minute to retrieve gifts they had left in the open—and by doing so, many lost their lives.

A supply convoy passes the ruins of the town of Ypres in Belgium.

A NEW YEAR OF WAR

The Christmas truce was over by the first week of 1915. Officers on both sides issued strict orders against any further unauthorized, peaceful contact with the enemy. Soldiers who fraternized could face a military trial or even a firing squad. Machine guns mowed down men who came out of their trenches for peaceful contact. In another symbol that Christmas was over, men in the British trenches who were short of ammunition began fashioning mortar shells out of their Princess Mary gift tins.

The fighting on the western front continued through the spring and summer. From December 1914 through March 1915, the French took the offensive in the Champagne region, around the ancient holy city of Reims where French kings had been crowned for centuries. There were other Allied offensives near the Belgian coast in the Yser region and around Verdun in the east. Despite the great expense of ammunition and soldiers, the Allies gained very little ground.

In April, the British began detonating huge explosive mines underneath the German trenches around Hill 60, southeast of Ypres. Thrown back by the explosions, the Germans were forced to surrender Hill 60 but gained it back with a counter-offensive in early May.

In the same sector, during what historians call the second battle of Ypres, the German army began using chlorine gas. The clouds of yellowish poison wafted on the breezes toward the lines of the British and French. The gas caused choking, suffocation, and paralysis of the lungs, leading to gruesome injuries and death. Men who climbed down into their trenches to avoid the gas suffered a quicker death—the substance was heavier than air and collected in trench bottoms and dugouts. Enemy rifles and machine guns shot down men who jumped out of their trenches to flee. The British responded with their first use of the gas at the battle of Loos in late September.

RISING WARTIME ANGER

Despite the Christmas truce and the frontline stalemate, political leaders remained opposed to any talk of peace. Their attitude was mirrored by civilian opinion, which was molded by newspapers' never-ending stream of horror stories. Through these articles, newspaper owners in London sought to inspire

The year 1915 saw the first use of poison chlorine gas in warfare.

A French newspaper illustrates a German submarine sinking a French fishing boat, just one example of the press highlighting the enemies' atrocities.

patriotic support for the war and an implacable hatred of the enemy. As a bonus, war generally brought higher circulation numbers and improved revenues. Readers were riveted by the war coverage.

The media gave prominent play to enemy atrocities, as well as the work of German submarines that were attacking merchant ships and threatening passenger liners in the North Atlantic. On May 7, 1915, the largest of these ships, the RMS *Lusitania*, was steaming eastward off the southern coast of Ireland towards its scheduled arrival in Liverpool, England. The German submarine U-20 stealthily approached beneath the waves. The encounter was sheer luck for the German crew, whose submarine could not match the ocean liner's speed, much less succeed in a chase. The captain of the U-20 gave the order to attack. A single torpedo struck the *Lusitania*'s starboard side, and the ship sank in 18 minutes. The death toll was high: nearly 1,200 civilian passengers and crew perished, including more than 120 Americans.[1] The United States was trying to stay neutral in the war, but Germany's attack on a civilian

AN EXECUTION ANGERS THE BRITISH

In August 1915, the Germans arrested British nurse Edith Cavell for harboring Allied soldiers. Caught behind the lines in Belgium when the German invasion occurred, Cavell gave British and Belgian soldiers shelter in her house and eventually helped them return to their units. Despite appeals from the British government and the neutral American government, she was executed by firing squad on October 12. The execution was played up widely in the British press and hardened British opinion against Germany.

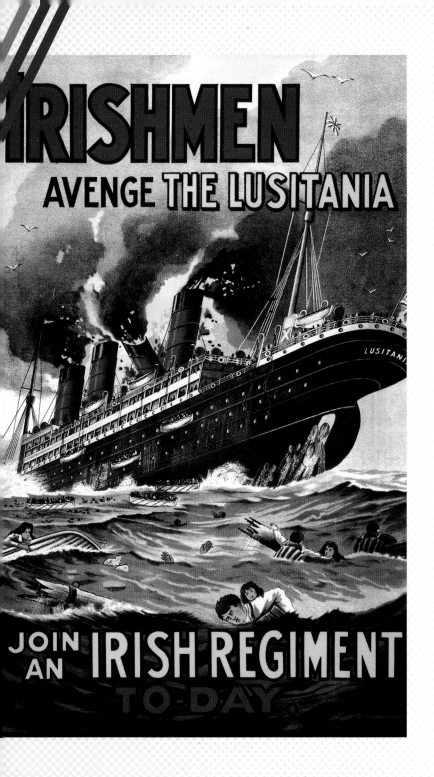

IRISHMEN AVENGE THE LUSITANIA

LUSITANIA

JOIN AN IRISH REGIMENT TO-DAY

ship swayed many Americans to side with the Allies. The country made no official declaration of war at the time, however.

Newspapers reported in November that Pope Benedict XV was once again trying to arrange a winter truce. This time, to convince the Russian government to take part, the Pope declared a truce among all Catholic and Orthodox nations. It would not be tied to Christmas—Catholic or Orthodox—or any other particular date.

The plea fell on deaf ears. The governments of Germany, France, the United Kingdom, and Russia expressed no interest in a winter truce, or any other attempts at a formal cease-fire.

Anger over the sinking of the *Lusitania* was used in British army recruitment posters to encourage men to volunteer.

The warring nations had been stationed in their trenches for more than a year. Casualties were heavy. Bitterness toward the enemy hardened attitudes among soldiers and officers of all levels. An explanation appeared in the *Edinburgh Evening News* on December 21, 1915:

> *To judge by statements made by soldiers home on leave from the Western front there is not much likelihood that this year will see the repetition of the informal truce between the combatants observed last Christmas. Feeling against the enemy is much more bitter than it was a year ago because of the adoption of poison gas [and] the submarine outrages . . . and our men seem to dislike the idea of any form or respite for men associated with such crimes. Those of the enemy who have been asked their views on the subject have answered frankly enough that a truce is forbidden by their commanders, except with the Belgians.*[2]

TRUCES AND MUTINIES

Although officers on both sides ordered that there should be no repeat of the 1914 Christmas truce, antiwar feeling spread among soldiers and civilians as the war continued. In 1917, for example, an uprising among Russian soldiers and sailors sparked a revolution that overthrew the czar and the Russian monarchy. Nearly half of the French infantry divisions mutinied against suicide assaults and bad conditions in the spring of 1917. In 1918, a widespread worker's strike in Germany pressured the government to end the war, eventually forcing Kaiser Wilhelm to leave the country.

The first American troops arrived in France in 1917, but US troops did not go into battle on a large scale until the spring of 1918.

PEACE AND AFTERMATH

Neither side would gain much ground on the western front until the summer and fall of 1918. Enormous battles took place along the Somme River and at Verdun to the southeast in 1916. In April 1917, the United States entered the war and began sending troops to the western front. As one ally entered, another left. Russia withdrew from the war in 1917 as a political revolution brought chaos and civil war conditions to Saint Petersburg, its capital.

Attitudes had hardened on both sides of the line. There seemed little chance of peace without a decisive battle. Some believed the war would go on forever, each side stuck pushing against the other and never gaining the upper hand. British Second Lieutenant Edward Beddington-Behrens wrote a letter home on December 26, 1916:

Everything was done to prevent any fraternizing between the two sides as the Boche [Germans] would use the opportunity by getting useful information. Besides, things have got past the stage when one can fraternize with the enemy, there is too much hatred flying about.[1]

But in some places, truces arose from the tactical situation. The lines were so close together, and activity so clearly visible, that any sniping would have touched off a major battle. Another frontline soldier described it as:

A curious situation as being so close to the Boche and so much above him, we looked down right into his trenches and could see every movement, while we for our part had to cross the sky line to get to our front line. By common consent there was a sort of policy of live and let live and neither side was sniped. If either of us had begun to use our rifles, both front lines would have become untenable.[2]

In many sectors, both sides restrained their artillery from attacking food depots. If a shell destroyed the rations for a mile of trench, there was sure to be retaliation—and both sides would go hungry. A philosophy of live and let live emerged despite the best efforts of commanding officers to bring about maximum death and destruction.

British officer Lieutenant Colonel Rowland Fielding had accepted a German-offered truce to rescue his wounded. Shortly afterward, he received an

Troops on both sides were weary of fighting and the terrible conditions of trench warfare.

order from higher-ups strictly forbidding any future negotiation or truces with the enemy, on pain of a court-martial. He wrote home in 1917:

> *In future, if fifty of our wounded are lying in No Man's Land, they are (as before) to remain there till dark, when we may get them in if we can; but no assistance, tacit or otherwise, is to be accepted from the enemy. Ruthlessness is to be the order of the day. Frightfulness is to be our watchword. Sportsmanship, chivalry, pity—all the qualities which Englishmen used to pride themselves in possessing—are to be scrapped.*[3]

To Fielding and many other officers, the war was becoming absurd. The British had mobilized for the sake of national honor and now were taking part in a senseless slaughter. There was no possible good outcome for either side.

THE ARMISTICE

On March 21, 1918, the German army started a new offensive on the western front. This attack, also known as the Saint Michael Offensive, broke the stalemate, but not in the way the Germans had hoped. The Allies threw back the assault, began seizing towns, and regained large swaths of territory. Many German regiments were forced to abandon their trenches and retreat.

A new invention, the armored tank, had appeared on the front in 1916 and had made its first significant impact in battles a year later. Allied tanks were a formidable force by 1918. These motorized gun platforms climbed over and around German trenches, causing havoc behind the lines. Although Kaiser Wilhelm had started the war with the best-equipped army in Europe, the loss of troops and war material on two fronts, as well as a strangling blockade imposed by the British navy, took their toll on the German economy. By this time many factory laborers had been called up for military service. The country's public finances were under strain, and German factories could not match British tank production. Frontline soldiers did not have the proper weapons to deal with tanks.

DEADLY ARTIFACTS OF WAR

The fighting on the western front left scars that have still not healed. In northern France and Belgium, shell holes and trenches left deep depressions in the ground, and the use of poison gas permanently contaminated many acres of farmland. Experts estimate 1.5 billion shells were launched during the war. Because of the soft, muddy ground, many of these bombs did not explode.

Farmers in Belgium routinely turn up unexploded shells even a century after the war's end. They dump the explosives at collection points for pickup by the Explosive Ordinance Deposit Company. This unit, a part of the Belgian army, has the job of clearing away and disposing of live and dud shells, grenades, and poison gas canisters found by farmers, hikers, and construction workers. Twenty members of the company have been killed in the line of duty, and in the area around Ypres there have been 358 civilian deaths and 535 civilian injuries caused by unexploded ordnance since the guns fell silent in 1918.[4]

The defeat on the western front demoralized the German commanders, who persuaded Wilhelm to ask for peace terms from the Allies. On November 11, 1918, the war ended with an armistice signed in the forest of Compiègne, north of Paris. Germany was forced to accept a full retreat of its army, the surrender of Alsace-Lorraine, and humiliating terms for a permanent peace. Kaiser Wilhelm had already lost power, giving up the throne on November 9 and fleeing to the Netherlands on November 10. The government of Austria-Hungary had dissolved earlier in the fall.

THE WAR SURVIVES

Bitter feelings lingered in the aftermath of World War I. Many British still believed Germany posed a threat to more "civilized" nations in Europe. Yet many ex-soldiers, who had seen the war from a different perspective, felt differently. A member of the British parliament and a veteran of the Christmas truce, Sir H. Kingsley Wood shared his thoughts during a debate in the House of Commons in 1930:

I . . . came to the conclusion that I have held very firmly ever since, that if we had been left to ourselves there would never have been another shot fired. For a fortnight the truce went on. We were on the most friendly terms, and it was only the fact that we were being controlled by others that made it necessary for us to start trying to shoot one another again.[5]

Crowds in New York City and throughout Allied nations celebrated Germany's surrender and the end of the war.

HUMAN TOLL

WAR COSTS IN LIVES

World War I cost its participants more casualties than in any previous war. On any given day of the war, hundreds died on the western front alone. The deadliest day was July 1, 1916, when 57,470 British soldiers alone died during the battle of the Somme. Beyond troop losses, experts estimate 13 million civilian deaths from disease, starvation, military action, and massacres.[6]

WORLD WAR I TROOP CASUALTIES BY COUNTRY, MAJOR COMBATANTS[7]

COUNTRY	KILLED	WOUNDED	PRISONERS/ MISSING	TOTAL
Russia	1,700,000	4,950,000	2,500,000	9,150,000
British Empire	908,371	2,090,212	191,652	3,190,235
France	1,357,800	4,266,00	537,000	6,160,800
Italy	650,000	947,000	600,000	2,197,000
United States	116,516	204,002	4,500	323,018
Germany	1,773,700	4,216,058	1,152,800	7,142,558
Austria-Hungary	1,200,000	3,620,000	2,200,000	7,020,000
Turkey	325,000	400,000	250,000	975,000
War Total (including all combatants)	8,528,831	21,189,154	7,750,919	37,466,904

The war had resulted in millions of casualties and widespread devastation. The bombardments and street fighting leveled hundreds of towns in northern France and Belgium. Heavy shelling and poison gas contaminated millions of acres of productive farmland.

The economic effects of the war were disastrous. For years, the people of France, the United Kingdom, and Germany suffered unemployment, hunger, and disease. Poor sanitation, overburdened hospitals, and the movement of soldiers along the fronts and across the Atlantic gave rise to a global influenza epidemic that killed more people than four years of fighting.

A peace conference held at Versailles in France set difficult terms on Germany, which was forced to pay heavy reparations to the Allies for the damages of the war. The German economy collapsed, and Germany went through a period of steep inflation that made the currency worthless and the most basic goods ridiculously expensive.

Many Germans believed they had been betrayed by their own leaders and stabbed in the back by war opponents at the front and within the country. Anger and a thirst for revenge gave rise to Adolf Hitler and the Nazi Party, which came to power in 1933. Hitler defied the Versailles treaty, rearmed Germany, and seized territory Germany had lost in 1918. In September 1939, Germany invaded Poland and launched another great war.

ADOLF HITLER

1889–1945

Adolf Hitler had been working as a painter in Vienna, Austria, when the war broke out. An enthusiastic volunteer, he moved up to the rank of corporal. Superior officers commended Hitler for his dedicated service, though he seemed to make few friends. Eventually he won a prestigious German medal, the Iron Cross First Class, for bravery under fire.

Hitler did not approve of the Christmas truce, and he believed any fraternization with the enemy was a stain on German honor. He is quoted in several accounts as declaring, "Something like this should not even be up for discussion during wartime."[8]

The armistice made him bitterly angry. Believing Germany's leaders had betrayed it, he resolved to give up his career as a painter and go into politics. After seizing control of the National Socialist German Worker's Party, also known as the Nazi Party, Hitler won appointment as the German chancellor in January 1933. He plunged the world into a second world war with an attack on Poland in 1939. World War II lasted from 1939 until 1945. With his empire in ruins and his enemies closing in, Hitler committed suicide in a bunker in Berlin, Germany, on April 30, 1945.

OTHER TRUCES, OTHER WARS

There would be no truces at Christmas or any other holiday season during World War II. But there were short episodes of fraternization at Tobruk, Libya, in 1941, and at Monte Cassino, Italy, in 1943. After a battle, it was common for both sides to stop firing and allow Red Cross orderlies to move about freely, claiming the dead and rescuing the wounded. These incidents were more common when conditions were similar to those of World War I: unchanging front lines, trench warfare, and opposing sides living in close proximity.

The international sport of soccer also provided the grounds for a truce in 1969 as the Nigerian army suppressed a violent uprising in the region of Biafra. A 48-hour truce was called while the Santos team from Brazil, which had on its roster the world-famous player Pelé, visited Nigeria for a friendly match. Men from both sides went to the game. Those remaining on the front listened to the match on the radio.

A SOCCER MATCH IN KABUL

On a dusty airfield in Kabul, Afghanistan, British and German troops dashed and scrambled around a soccer ball. It was December 25, 2014, the one-hundredth anniversary of the Christmas Truce. The soldiers were fighting side-by-side as part of a coalition sent to keep the peace in the Afghan capital. The match ended with a British victory, 3–0.

German and British soldiers serving together in Afghanistan played soccer in December 2014 to celebrate the one-hundredth anniversary of the Christmas Truce.

The Christmas truce was later celebrated by movies, plays, and books. It has inspired television ads and commemorative soccer matches that marked the one-hundredth anniversary of the event. In the view of many historians, it serves as a modern example of chivalric warfare. In the Middle Ages, combatants would suspend fighting on holy days or on certain days of the week. Opposing knights would take part in jousts, contests of skill and strength on horseback. During the Crusades, a general truce was called throughout Europe to allow Christians to unite in an effort to capture the holy city of Jerusalem from the Muslim Turks.

Since World War I, the notions of medieval chivalry have largely been left behind during warfare. Trench warfare has become obsolete, and opposing soldiers rarely see each other on the battlefield. Nevertheless, the nations of the world still claim to honor an international code of conduct dating to 1864, known as the Geneva Convention, on the treatment of wartime prisoners. In addition, war crimes can be punished by courts of law and by the International Criminal Court, which sits in The Hague, Netherlands. And the personal honor and mutual trust shown for two days on the terrible battlefields of World War I inspires a sense of hope for a more peaceful future.

Modern memorials remind viewers of the peaceful and civilized message of the Christmas truce.

TIMELINE

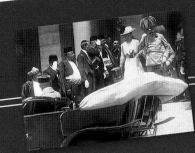

June 28, 1914

Serbian nationalist Gavrilo Princip assassinates Austrian Archduke Franz Ferdinand in Sarajevo.

July 23, 1914

Austria presents a list of demands to Serbia to make amends for the assassination of the archduke.

August 2, 1914

Germany demands the Belgian government allow German armies to freely cross its territory.

August 4, 1914

Germany invades Belgium.

December 20, 1914

Indian troops fail to throw back German units in the Battle of Givenchy.

December 24, 1914

German and British troops agree to informal truces in France and Belgium.

December 25, 1914

The Christmas truces continue throughout the day.

May 7, 1915

A German submarine sinks the passenger liner *Lusitania* during a voyage from New York to Liverpool.

September 1914

The German offensive along the Marne River is halted by the French.

October 29, 1914

Belgian engineers flood a large swath of low-lying countryside and stop German assaults against British positions.

December 7, 1914

Pope Benedict XV calls for a holiday truce to begin.

December 19, 1914

The British begin an offensive at Ploegsteert Wood.

April 1917

The United States enters the war.

March 21, 1918

Germany begins a wide-ranging offensive along the western front.

November 11, 1918

Germany surrenders, and France and Britain agree to an armistice.

December 25, 2014

British and German troops in Afghanistan play soccer to remember the Christmas truce.

ESSENTIAL FACTS

KEY PLAYERS

- Herbert H. Asquith was prime minister of the United Kingdom. In the summer of 1914, Asquith favored military support of Belgium in case of an invasion by Germany, a stance that brought the British into the war.

- Kaiser Wilhelm was the leader of Germany who declared war in 1914 believing his nation was under threat from France, the United Kingdom, and Russia.

- Marshal Joseph Joffre was the French military commander at the start of World War I who led a counterattack at the First Battle of the Marne that stopped the German army before it could reach Paris.

- Czar Nicholas II was the ruler of Russia in 1914 who sought to avoid a large-scale mobilization at the start of World War I but was overruled by his advisers.

KEY STATISTICS

- The German military sent more than one million men to the western front.

- The British government sent 355,000 Princess Mary gift boxes to its troops to mark Christmas 1914.

- Kaiser Wilhelm of Germany sent 100,000 Christmas trees to his troops on the western front for Christmas 1914.

IMPACT ON HISTORY

The 1914 Christmas truces of World War I had little impact on the war and generally stopped in later years. Today they are considered a reminder of how humanity can reemerge in the midst of bloodshed.

QUOTE

"Next morning the mist was slow to clear and suddenly my orderly threw himself into my dugout to say that both German and Scottish soldiers had come out of their trenches and were fraternizing along the front. I grabbed my binoculars and looking cautiously over the parapet saw the incredible sight of our soldiers exchanging cigarettes, schnapps and chocolate with the enemy. Later a Scottish soldier appeared with a football."

—*Lieutenant Johannes Niemann of the German 133rd Saxon Regiment*

GLOSSARY

ARMISTICE
A temporary stop of fighting by mutual agreement.

ARTILLERY
Large guns manned by a crew of operators used to shoot long distances.

DUGOUT
A room built into the side of a trench, used for protection from enemy fire and the weather.

FRATERNIZATION
The cessation of fighting in order to mingle with enemy soldiers or civilians in an enemy country.

INFANTRY
Soldiers who fight on foot; the branch of the army including these soldiers.

INSURGENT
A person who fights against a government or other authority.

MOBILIZATION
Calling up troops for immediate training and shipment to the war fronts.

NO-MAN'S-LAND
The dangerous territory lying between opposing trenches targeted by artillery and snipers and lined with barbed wire obstructions to slow enemy advances.

PARAPET

A low wall, especially at the edge of a wall or platform.

PROPAGANDA

Information used to support a political group or point of view, or to persuade the audience to support their country's participation in a war.

RECONNAISSANCE

An exploration of an area to gather information about the activity of military forces.

REPARATION

Compensation required from a defeated nation for damage or injury during a war.

SAPPER

A soldier trained for demolition missions and underground mining of enemy trenches.

SNIPER

An infantry rifleman whose task is to kill individual enemy soldiers at long range.

STALEMATE

A draw or a position between opponents in which neither side can get an advantage or win.

ADDITIONAL RESOURCES

SELECTED BIBLIOGRAPHY

Brown, Malcolm, and Shirley Seaton. *The Christmas Truce*. London: Papermac, 1994. Print.

Hastings, Max. *Catastrophe 1914: Europe Goes to War*. New York: Knopf, 2013. Print.

Keegan, John. *An Illustrated History of the First World War*. New York: Knopf, 2001. Print.

Neiberg, Michael S. *Fighting the Great War: A Global History*. Cambridge, MA: Harvard UP, 2006. Print.

Weintraub, Stanley. *Silent Night: The Story of the World War I Christmas Truce*. New York: Free Press, 2001. Print.

FURTHER READINGS

Porter, Phil. *The Christmas Truce*. London, UK: Oberon, 2014. Print.

Pratt, Mary K. *World War I*. Minneapolis, MN: Abdo, 2014.

Tuchman, Barbara W. *The Guns of August*. New York: Presidio, 2004. Print.

WEBSITES

To learn more about Essential Library of World War I, visit **booklinks.abdopublishing.com**. These links are routinely monitored and updated to provide the most current information available.

PLACES TO VISIT

Imperial War Museum
Lambeth Road
London SE1 6HZ
United Kingdom
+44 20 7416 5000
http://www.iwm.org.uk/
The Imperial War Museum includes major exhibitions on World War I and other conflicts involving the United Kingdom and its colonies.

National World War I Museum
100 W. Twenty-Sixth Street
Kansas City, MO 64108
816-888-8100
https://theworldwar.org/contact-us
The museum offers photographs, exhibitions, uniforms, and artifacts from the war, as well as an online exhibition on the Christmas truce.

SOURCE NOTES

CHAPTER 1. PEACE BREAKS OUT

1. Adrian Lee. "The Battle to Feed Tommy: New Exhibition Looks at the Diet of a WW1 Soldier." *Express*. Northern and Shell Media, 23 Aug. 2014. Web. 30 June 2015.

2. Ernest Junger. *The Storm of Steel: From the Diary of a German Storm-Troop Officer on the Western Front.* London: Chatto and Windus, 1929. Print. 192.

3. Stanley Weintraub. *Silent Night: The Story of the World War I Christmas Truce.* New York: Free Press, 2001. Print. 6–7.

4. Malcolm Brown and Shirley Seaton. *Christmas Truce.* London: Papermac, 1994. Print. 32.

5. Gerry Carroll. "Christmas Truce—November 1914 to New Years Eve 1914." *John Minnery MC, DCM, MM.* Gerry Carroll, n.d. Web. 30 June 2015.

6. Mike Dash. "The Story of the WWI Christmas Truce." *Smithsonian Magazine*. Smithsonian Institution, 23 Dec. 2011. Web. 20 June 2015.

CHAPTER 2. THE GREAT WAR

1. Michael S. Neiberg. *Fighting the Great War: A Global History.* Cambridge, MA: Harvard UP, 2006. Print. 1.

2. John Keegan. *An Illustrated History of the First World War.* New York: Knopf, 2001. Print. 52.

3. Michael S. Neiberg. *Fighting the Great War: A Global History.* Cambridge, MA: Harvard UP, 2006. Print. 12.

4. Peter Englund and Peter Graves. *The Beauty and the Sorrow: An Intimate History of the First World War.* New York: Vintage, 2012. Print. 9.

5. John Keegan. *An Illustrated History of the First World War.* New York: Knopf, 2001. Print. 67.

6. Herbert Asquith. "British Prime Minister Herbert Asquith's Address to Parliament, 6 August 1914." *Source Records of the Great War, Vol. I*, ed. Charles F. Horne. N.p.: National Alumni, 1923. *firstworldwar.com*. Web. 20 June 2015.

7. "How Did Britain Let 250,000 Underage Soldiers Fight in WW1?" *BBC*. BBC, n.d. Web. 30 June 2015.

CHAPTER 3. APPEALS FOR PEACE

1. Michael S. Neiberg. *Fighting the Great War: A Global History*. Cambridge, MA: Harvard UP, 2006. Print. 12.

2. Ibid. 13.

3. Terry Cudbird. *Walking the Retreat: The March to the Marne: 1914 Revisited*. Oxford, UK: Signal, 2014. 12. *Google Book Search*. Web. 30 June 2015.

4. Ian Summer. *The First Battle of the Marne, 1914: The French "Miracle" Halts the Germans*. Oxford, UK: Osprey, 2010. Print. 38.

5. Chris Baker. "The Christmas Truce of 1914." *The Long, Long Trail*. Chris Baker/Milverton Associates, n.d. Web. 30 June 2015.

6. Sigmund Freud. "Thoughts for the Times on War and Death." 1915. *Freud Museum London*. PDF. 30 June 2015.

CHAPTER 4. THE CHRISTMAS SEASON

1. "Princess Mary Tobacco Box Owned by Captain Charles A Ogden, 1st Battalion, the Bedfordshire Regiment, 1914." *National Army Museum*. National Army Museum, 2015. Web. 30 June 2015.

2. Malcolm Brown and Shirley Seaton. *Christmas Truce*. London: Papermac, 1994. Print. 40.

3. Gary G. Kohls. "World War I: Lessons from the Christmas Truce of 1914." *Global Research Centre for Research on Globalization*. Global Research, 9 Nov. 2014. Web. 30 June 2015.

4. Malcolm Brown and Shirley Seaton. *Christmas Truce*. London: Papermac, 1994. Print. 39.

5. Max Hastings. *Catastrophe, 1914: Europe Goes to War*. New York: Knopf, 2001. 541.

6. Stanley Weintraub. *Silent Night: The Story of the World War I Christmas Truce*. New York: Free Press, 2001. Print. 33.

7. Associated Press. "Alfred Anderson, 109, Last Man from 'Christmas Truce' of 1914, Dies." *New York Times*. New York Times, 22 Nov. 2005. Web. 30 June 2015.

8. "Football with the Enemy." *The Times*. Times Newspapers Limited, 31 Dec. 2014. Web. 30 June 2015.

9. "The Winter Operations 1914–1915." *The Long, Long Trail*. Chris Baker/Milverton Associates, n.d. Web. 30 June 2015.

CHAPTER 5. CHRISTMAS MEALS AND SOCCER MATCHES

1. "Officer's Story. An Informal Compact for the Day." *Birmingham Daily Mail*, 31 Dec. 1914. "Christmas Truce 1914." *Worldwide Genealogy*. Web. 30 June 2015.

2. Malcolm Brown and Shirley Seaton. *Christmas Truce*. London: Papermac, 1994. Print. 39.

3. Edward Hamilton Westrow Hulse. *Letters Written from the English Front in France between September 1914 and March 1915*. Privately printed, 1916. *Internet Archive*. Web. 30 June 2015.

4. Malcolm Brown and Shirley Seaton. *Christmas Truce*. London: Papermac, 1994. Print. 99.

5. Robert M. Sapolsky. "The Spirit of the 1914 Christmas Truce." *Wall Street Journal*. Wall Street Journal, 19 Dec. 2014. Web. 30 June 2015.

6. "Halfway Meeting. English and Germans Exchange Souvenirs." *Birmingham Gazette*, 31 Dec. 1914. "Christmas Truce 1914." *Worldwide Genealogy*. Web. 30 June 2015.

7. Stanley Weintraub. *Silent Night: The Story of the World War I Christmas Truce*. New York: Free Press, 2001. Print. 83.

8. Simon Kuper. "Soccer in the Trenches: Remembering the World War I Christmas Truce." *ESPN FC*. ESPN, 23 Dec. 2014. Web. 30 June 2015.

9. Malcolm Brown and Shirley Seaton. *Christmas Truce*. London: Papermac, 1994. Print. 138–139.

10. James Masters. "WWI Christmas Truce Football Match: Fact or Fiction?" *CNN*. CNN, 25 Dec. 2014. Web. 30 June 2015.

CHAPTER 6. CARRYING ON THE FIGHT

1. Stanley Weintraub. *Silent Night: The Story of the World War I Christmas Truce*. New York: Free Press, 2001. Print. 128.

2. "'Tipperary' Sung to Germans. Friends for a Day." *Manchester Courier and Lancashire General Advertiser*, 4 Jan. 1915. "Christmas Truce 1914." *Worldwide Genealogy*. Web. 30 June 2015.

3. Stanley Weintraub. *Silent Night: The Story of the World War I Christmas Truce*. New York: Free Press, 2001. Print. 136.

CHAPTER 7. A NEW YEAR OF WAR

1. A. A. Hoehling. *The Great War at Sea: A History of Naval Action, 1914–1918*. New York: Crowell, 1965. Print. 86.

2. "Christmas at the Front." *Edinburgh Evening News*, 21 Dec. 1915. "Christmas Truce 1914." *Worldwide Genealogy*. Web. 30 June 2015.

CHAPTER 8. PEACE AND AFTERMATH

1. Malcolm Brown and Shirley Seaton. *Christmas Truce*. London: Papermac, 1994. Print. 207.

2. Ibid. 208–209.

3. Ibid. 210.

4. Martin Fletcher. "Lethal Relics from WW1 are Still Emerging." *Telegraph*. Telegraph Media Group, 12 July 2013. Web. 30 June 2015.

5. John V. Denson. "The Christmas Truce of World War I." *Mises Institute*. Mises Institute, 25 Dec. 2012. Web. 30 June 2015.

6. "World War I." *Encyclopedia Britannica*. Encyclopedia Britannica, 2015. Web. 30 June 2015.

7. "WWI Casualty and Death Tables." *PBS*. Public Broadcasting Service, n.d. Web. 30 June 2015.

8. "New Evidence of First World War Christmas Truces Uncovered." *University of Aberdeen News*. University of Aberdeen, 15 Dec. 2010. Web. 30 June 2015.

INDEX

ABOUT THE AUTHOR

Tom Streissguth has worked as a journalist, teacher, law clerk, courier, and book editor, and he has published more than 100 works of nonfiction for many school and library publishers. A graduate of Yale University, he is the founder of The Archive, an independent publisher of historical journalism collections used by teachers, students, and researchers. He currently lives in Woodbury, Minnesota.